BOOKER T. WASHINGTON

Before the Civil War, Negroes in the South were slaves. Booker T. Washington had to work hard for the white man who owned him. After the war, Booker could go to school at night. He became a teacher so he could help other Negroes have better lives. Later he was the head of the first school in America that Negroes ran by themselves. This easy-to-read biography tells about a great man who was born a slave and who helped lead his people out of slavery.

BOOKER T. WASHINGTON

by WILLIAM WISE
Illustrations by PAUL FRAME

A
SEE and READ
BEGINNING TO READ
BIOGRAPHY

G. P. PUTNAM'S SONS   NEW YORK

*Nothing ever comes to one, that is worth
having, except as a result of hard work.*
— BOOKER T. WASHINGTON

SEE AND READ
Beginning to Read Biographies

ABRAHAM LINCOLN by Patricia Miles Martin
Illustrated by Gustav Schrotter

NATHAN HALE by Virginia Frances Voight
Illustrated by Frank Aloise

CHRISTOPHER COLUMBUS by Helen D. Olds
Illustrated by Al Davidson

CRAZY HORSE by Glen Dines
Illustrated by the Author

SAM HOUSTON by Paul Hollander
Illustrated by Salem Tamer

Copyright © 1968 by William Wise
All rights reserved. Published simultaneously in the
Dominion of Canada by Longmans Canada Limited, Toronto.
Library of Congress Catalog Card Number: 68-15087
PRINTED IN THE UNITED STATES OF AMERICA

07209

BOOKER T. WASHINGTON

Booker T. Washington was born in
Virginia in the year 1858.

He never knew his father. He lived
with his mother, an older brother, and a
sister. Their home was a tiny one-room
cabin on a plantation.

Booker and his family were slaves.
They belonged to the white man who
owned the plantation. In 1858 there were
many Negro slaves in the South. Negroes
who lived in the North were free.

Living was not easy or pleasant for Booker and his family. In the winter their tiny cabin was very cold. In the summer it was hot.

There were no beds in the cabin. At night Booker and his family went to sleep on the cabin floor.

All the slaves on the plantation had to
work hard. As soon as he was big
enough, Booker had to work hard, too.

Sometimes he filled a pail with water.
He carried the heavy pail out to the men
working in the fields.

Sometimes he took corn to the mill to
be ground. The mill was three miles
from the plantation. By the time he began
to ride back from the mill, it was dark.

Booker was afraid to ride alone
through the dark woods. But he had to
do it. There was no other way to get
back to the plantation.

The plantation owner had a little girl
who went to school. One day Booker
was told to carry her books for her.
When they got to school, she went inside.

Booker had to stay behind. In the
South, Negro children did not go to
school. Because of this, most Negroes in
the South did not know how to read.
Many did not even know how to write
their names.

Booker stood by the door and looked
inside. He could see the little girl and the
other white children at their schoolwork.

From that day on, he wanted to go
to school.

He wanted to learn how to read
and write.

When Booker was still very young, the
American Civil War began.

Men fight wars for many reasons. The
North and the South had many reasons
to fight the Civil War.

15

One reason was that the Northern
states wanted the Negroes in America to
be free. They wanted to end slavery.

The Southern states wanted to
keep slaves.

And so, for four terrible years, the war
went on.

One morning, when Booker was seven,
all the slaves on the plantation were
called away from work. They went to the
house where the plantation owner lived.

The plantation owner said the war was over. The North had won.

A soldier from the North was there. He read a long paper. It was President Abraham Lincoln's Emancipation Proclamation.

The Emancipation Proclamation said that there would never be any more slavery in America.

No man, woman, or child would
ever again belong to anyone else. The
Negroes in the South were free.

For a little while all the Negroes on
the plantation were very happy. Booker's
mother said that this was the day she
had always wanted to see. She cried
because she was so happy.

But soon Booker and his family grew sad. They knew that their troubles were not over. Now, because they were free, they had to think about things they had never thought about before.

'They had to think about where they would live.

They had to think about the work they would do.

They would need money to buy their
own food and clothing. They would need
money to buy everything else that free
people must buy for themselves.

In time, Booker's mother learned that
there was work to be had in West
Virginia. They put the few things they
owned into a cart. They tied a mule to
the cart. Then they began to follow the
road that ran over the mountains.

It was a very long trip. Booker walked
most of the way by the side of the cart.

When they got to West Virginia,
Booker found work in a coal mine. The
mine was very dark. It was very dirty.

The work was terrible for a child. But
Booker knew that his mother needed all
the money he could make. Because of
this, he worked in the coal mine from
morning till dark.

Booker still wanted to go to school, though. His mother wanted him to go, too. So he went at night, after his work in the coal mine was over.

There was only one teacher at the school. There were only two or three books.

Some of the students were children. Some of the students were men and women who had never been able to go to school before.

Booker learned as much as he could at
the little school. Then, one afternoon, he
heard two men talking in the coal mine.
They were talking about a big school in
Virginia, called the Hampton Institute.

The men said that the Hampton
Institute was a school for Negroes. A
poor boy like Booker could go there. He
could learn much more there than he
could ever learn at home.

That night Booker told his mother
what he had heard. He said that he
wanted to go to the Hampton Institute,
even though it was very far away.

For two years Booker saved all the money he could. His family tried to help him. So did the other Negroes in the town. They gave him their nickels and dimes. It was all the money they had to give.

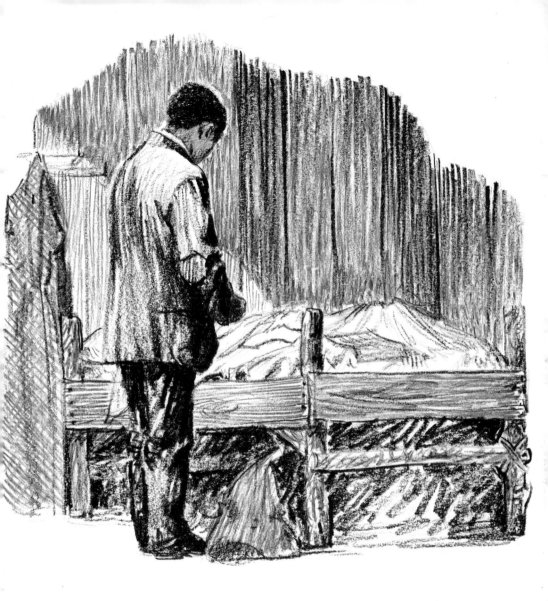

At last it was time to leave home. He
said good-bye to his friends and family.
His mother was old and sick. He didn't
know if he would ever see her again.

He made the first part of the trip by
stagecoach. One very cold night in the
mountains the stagecoach stopped at a
small hotel. The hotelkeeper would not
give Booker a room. No Negro, he said,
was ever going to sleep in *his* hotel.

All night Booker walked around
outside, trying to keep warm. He had
heard before that some white people in
America felt only hatred for Negroes.
But this was the first time he had ever
met such hatred face to face.

After crossing the mountains, Booker took a train to Richmond. When he got to the city, he had no money left.

He began to walk around the city. In a store window he saw some beautiful apple pies. But he had no money to buy one.

As it grew dark, he came to a low wooden bridge. Tired and hungry, he crawled under the bridge. The last thing he heard as he fell asleep was the noise of people walking on the wooden bridge over his head.

The next day he saw a ship down by
the water. The captain said he could
have a job carrying heavy boxes onto
the ship.

Booker worked this way for a week.
To save money, he slept each night
under the same wooden bridge. By the
end of the week he had saved enough
money to take a train to the Hampton
Institute.

The Hampton Institute was run by
General Samuel C. Armstrong. The
general had been a Northern soldier
during the Civil War. Now he wanted to
help the white and Negro peoples of the
South as much as he could.

Booker T. Washington stayed at Hampton for three years. He learned to read very hard books. He learned to speak well before other people and to make them listen to what he said.

Great men cultivate love, only little men cherish a spirit of hatred

He learned another thing at Hampton. He was going to become a teacher and help other Negroes find a better place in the world.

For two years he worked as a
schoolteacher in West Virginia. Then
General Armstrong asked him to come
back to Hampton, to run the night
school there.

He ran the night school very well.
Before long the general knew that his
young friend, Booker T. Washington,
was ready for an even harder job.

One day a letter came for the general.
It said that a new school for Negroes
was to open in Tuskegee, Alabama.
Would the general help? Would he send
one of his teachers from Hampton to be
the head of the new school?

The general said he would send one of
the best teachers he had. He sent Booker
T. Washington.

For the rest of his days Booker T.
Washington was the head of the school
at Tuskegee. Tuskegee Institute became
very well known. It was the first great
school in America that Negroes ran by
themselves.

The students at Tuskegee learned many
things from books.

They learned how to make tables,
chairs, and beds for their homes.

They learned how to run a farm.
They learned what foods they should eat,
to keep strong and fit.

And they learned something else. They
learned to take pride in the school and
pride in themselves.

It was not an easy job to be the head
of Tuskegee Institute. The school was
always poor. Again and again Booker T.
Washington had to find more money.

He went to the North to tell the story
of Tuskegee. He told the story so well
that many rich men and women gave
him money for the school.

As the years went by, Tuskegee Institute became famous all over the world. Booker T. Washington became famous, too.

He had many friends in both the
North and the South. One spring some
of his friends saw that he was tired.
They said he needed a rest. They gave
him a ticket and sent him to Europe on
a ship. It was his first rest in almost
twenty years.

Everywhere he went, people wanted to meet him. They wanted to meet the man who had been born a slave and who had become so famous.

In England he went to Windsor Castle,
to have tea with Queen Victoria. She
asked him about Tuskegee. She asked him
about slavery. She asked him the same
questions that other people had asked
him — even though she *was* a famous
queen.

After his trip Booker T. Washington
came home again. He worked hard at
Tuskegee for many years more.

Maybe he worked *too* hard. In 1915,
when he died, many people thought it
was from overwork.

No man can always please everyone. Booker T. Washington did not please everyone either. After he died, there were people who said that Tuskegee Institute might have been a better school than it was.

A few people said that Booker T. Washington should have thought things that he did not think. They said he should have done things that he did not do.

Most people, though, said that Booker
T. Washington had been a great man.
He had built a wonderful school at
Tuskegee. He had given pride to many
of his race. Most people will always
remember him for these things. They
will remember him as the man who was
born a slave and who helped lead
America's Negroes out of slavery.

KEY WORDS

cabin
cart
Civil War
coal mine
Emancipation
  Proclamation
famous
free
Hampton Institute
hatred
hotel

job
mule
Negro
owner
plantation
pride
slave
slavery
soldier
stagecoach
student

Tuskegee Institute

The Author

WILLIAM WISE is the author of a number of See and Read Beginning to Read Books, including *Franklin Delano Roosevelt, Monsters of Today and Yesterday, The World of Giant Mammals,* and *Sir Howard the Coward.* For older readers, Mr. Wise has written *The Two Reigns of Tutankhamen,* which received a Boys' Clubs of America Junior Book Award Medal, and *Alexander Hamilton,* a Junior Literary Guild Selection.

The Artist

PAUL FRAME lives in New York City, where he is active in many phases of educational work at the Friends Seminary. He has illustrated biographies of Franklin Delano Roosevelt, Eleanor Roosevelt, John Fitzgerald Kennedy, Lyndon Baines Johnson, and Henry Ford, as well as *The Boy with One Shoe, Honestly, Katie John!,* and *Casey at the Bat.*